90sHT
xoMTG is an imprint of Big Green Machine Group LLC
www.xomtg.com

This book was inspired by the song and music video 90sHT
performed by Nasya Marie featuring Life of Zhae and directed by Dana Rice.

Text copyright@2019 by Nasya Marie | www.nasyamarie.com
Illustration copyright@2019 by Mark Weems | @dolothegoat
Photography copyright@2019 by Dana Rice | www.danariceproductions.com

A portion of the music video 90sHT was shot at Rose Studios
located in Los Angeles, California | www.rosestudiosla.com

Artistic Direction provided by Nikole Butler | www.nikolebutler.com

All rights reserved. No part of this publication may be reproduced, distributed, or transmitted in any form or by any means, including photocopying, recording, or other electronic or mechanical methods, without the prior written permission of the publisher except in the case of brief quotations embodied in reviews and certain other non-commercial uses permitted by copyright law.

xoMTG
a division of Big Green Machine Group LLC
4132 E Joppa Road, Suite 110
Baltimore, Maryland 21236

90sHT, Nasya Marie, xoMTG and the xoMTG Heart are registered trademarks of
Big Green Machine Group LLC.

Paperback ISBN 978-1-7331769-2-7
eBook ISBN 978-1-7331769-4-1

Library of Congress Control Number: 2019953315

ATTENTION
Schools, Businesses, Book Clubs and Groups: xoMTG offers quantity discounts with bulk purchase for business, educational or promotional use. For more information, contact connect@xomtg.com

First Special Collector's Edition

This book is a part of a multi-media
release entitled 90sHT.
The multimedia release includes a book,
a song, and a music video
with the same title by Nasya Marie.
www.nasyamarie.com

The Nasya Marie clothing collection
is available on
www.xomachinethegreen.com

From one HeartThrob to another,

Thank you for reading my book.
It means a lot.
I hope you feel inspired.
I hope you gain insight
on the things that matter the most.
I hope you feel loved,
empowered and encouraged.

xo, go get it
Nasya Marie

Dedicated to
The HeartThrobs
inspired by '90s Hip Hop

To my mother
for teaching me about the most important things in life
while growing into a young woman.
-Nasya Marie

To the youth and to young entrepreneurs
-Mark Weems

To Karin Ganser
-Dana Rice

Everything is everything may not be a saying that everyone says anymore, but it's still a relevant and important message.
As a young person, I might be underestimated, misunderstood, or not taken seriously. But it doesn't make me, or my purpose, any less important than someone with millions of dollars or 20 cars. I can get anything done that I set my mind to accomplish. It may not be easy, fast or comfortable, but *everything is everything*. All of the hard work and tears will pay off in the end.

"Everything is everything, what is meant to be, will be."
-Lauryn Hill 1998

What does success look like to you?

How have your challenges molded you into the person you are
today?

We know we've got it going on.
They like our style, and they copy it.
We are going to go ahead and "do us",
because no one can "do us"
better than we can.
Let's stunt on em' shall we?

Hard Core

"You got it goin' on"- Lil' Kim '96

What is your style? How does it make you unique?

Write a list of 10 things that make you different.

"You run like a girl"
yeah, I do, and?
"You can't do that you're a lady"
Ok?
"Stay in your lane, that's a man's job."
Oh really?
Watch me do it.

"Why would you wear that?
You don't wanna call attention to yourself"

Whatever

What are your thoughts on women's rights?

Do you think that society's outlook on women has changed since the women's suffrage movement began in 1848?

What are your thoughts on "womanism"?

Look up the term "womanism", a term created by the author and activist Alice Walker in her book "In Search of Our Mother's Garden". Is her outlook on the Black woman's experience still relevant today?

Some call it drugs.
For some, it's an attitude.
It's how you walk and talk.
It's a lifestyle.

We are

Dope

List things about yourself that make you dope.

96 Heart Throb

Being unique means we are going to stick out like a sore thumb, but we are more than enough. Period. People are going to criticize us and tell us how to be us 24/7 and we will no longer tolerate it, or change, because of other people's opinions anymore.

Why would we change for someone else if we could be

Slicker than
your
average?

How are you slicker than
the average?

Because I'm a female, I have to fit the status quo of not being too small or too big. Too loud or too quiet.
Too much or too little.
Because I'm black, I have to accept being objectified, belittled, and being called names that are usually unaccepted.
I am expected to be perfect
in order to be successful?
You're trippin, because I am Human,
and the only perfection
that I'm striving for
is to be completely loved and accepted by me
That's what makes me perfect.

Trippin'

Do you allow other people's opinions to influence you?

Name some things that people criticize you about. How do you feel about it?

Expressing my self-love is cocky?
Taking care of my mental health is taboo?
Taking time to love myself
before I love someone else
is uncalled for?

I can dress how I want.
(as long as I'm not distracting).
I can be myself.
(as long as I'm not weird)

So, it's okay that every move I make as a young woman, a human being, is criticized?

You're Buggin'

Why is caring for your mental health important?

What can you do to take care of your mental health?

96 Heart Throb

Our ancestors
worked hard for us so that we could have the
opportunities that we have today.
We must know who we are, and
we are constantly changing for the better.
We are free to shape our futures.
We are walking in the power of the love we
hold inside because,

We're Cool Like That

Why do you think the '90s were important?

Do you feel like
the contributions that your
grandparents or parents made were important? Why?

"I'm Bout it Bout it"
-Master P '96

I'm ready to get it done.
I'm ready to do what I need to do.
I don't need your approval,
your green light
or your label.

I'm investing in my future

Do you think it's important to invest in yourself?

Name some steps that you can take
to invest in
yourself.

Write down 5 goals you want to accomplish
in the next 5 years.

96 Heart Throb

WAZZZUUUPPP!
-Martin Lawrence, 1992

Wazzup is one of those feelings.
That moment when you see your friend.

That moment when you know the culture is alive and well. Without hip-hop culture, we wouldn't even greet each other with

wazzup

It may just seem like a word to some, but it validates our identity and love for one another.

Name the
people who you love you.

Take a moment to reflect and think about
how you can spend more time and appreciate them.

"You're mine."
"You belong to me."

Don't play yourself

I am not your property

Why is it important to take ownership of yourself?

Have you been in a relationship where someone made you feel like property?

Just because a rumor starts about us,
someone comes for us on social media,
or someone prematurely judges us,
it doesn't mean we have to believe
what they say is true.
They don't know us.
It doesn't mean that we have to respond.
Actions speak louder than words.
If the time comes where we need to respond in our
truth to shut everything down, then

Holla Back!

Have you ever been involved in drama?

How did you handle it?
Did you rise above it?
How did it affect your mental health?

bling

We may not all say bling anymore,
but the word has evolved into different words
that mean the same thing.

Ice

drip

These words acknowledge the expensive
things that we own.
It makes us feel good.
It gives us something to show off.
It may even feel like we finally passed
a milestone of achievement,
but at the end of the day, we take the Bling off.
The same person before I bought this Bling
is still here.
It was an object
and these objects
should never define me.

Should you let materialistic things define you?

Why or why not?

thick

My thighs? thick.
My stretch marks? thick.
My Body? thick.
My personality? thick.
Who said that growing into a woman
was supposed to be perfect? Who is defining
what it means to be "perfect", anyway?
If I let other people define me,
then I will never be the "me"
I'm supposed to be.
I am
positively, unapologetically, and beautifully

thick

How are you thick?

Do you love being thick?

Why or why not?

A heartthrob in the past was always
this hot guy that all the girls swooned over.
That was the past.
I can be my own heartthrob.

"My first love is me, myself and I.
I am a heartthrob, all on my own."
- NasyaMarie

Do you love
yourself?

Should you love yourself before you
love someone else?

How are you
your own
heartthrob?

Stream and purchase my song
90sHT by Nasya Marie
featuring Life of Zhae
Watch my music video on Youtube
www.nasyamarie.com

Watch, like and subscribe
to our family Youtube Channel
and podcast
Our Big Green Life

Subscribe and listen to my podcast:
It's Me

Learn more about our company:
www.xomtg.com

Buy our merch and support our clothing line.
We make donations from every sale to
our community partners:
www.xomachinethegreen.com

www.ingramcontent.com/pod-product-compliance
Lightning Source LLC
Chambersburg PA
CBRC100024110526
44587CB00009BA/184